With All Flags Flying.

100 AMERICAN FLAGS

100 AMERICAN FLAGS

A UNIQUE COLLECTION OF OLD GLORY MEMORABILIA

COLLECTION & DESIGN BY KIT HINRICHS

TEXT BY DELPHINE HIRASUNA

PHOTOGRAPHY BY TERRY HEFFERNAN

TEN SPEED PRESS
Berkeley | Toronto

75 40

The Continental Congress resolved in 1777 that "the flag of the United States be thirteen stripes, alternate red and white; that the Union be thirteen stars, white in a blue field representing a new constellation." The Revolutionary War–time haste with which this resolution was written left these graphic elements open to broad interpretation. ★ Far from being a static symbol, the American flag has been rendered with stars in countless configurations, especially as a new star was added each time a state joined the Union. Not only did the "constellation" vary from circles to rows, gaps were left on the blue canton by practical flag makers anticipating additional stars as more territories earned statehood. ★ It was not until Congress passed official standards in 1912 that the flag took on a fixed appearance. Still, more than a century without guidelines established a tradition of personalizing the Stars and Stripes, letting it speak not just for a nation, but for an ideal, a value, a way of life. ★ Over the years, the American flag has been raised high in wartime triumph and peacetime celebration; burned in fervent protest; shown proudly on quilts, pillowcases, and bags; appropriated by commercial interests to sell goods; and honored every Fourth of July to celebrate America's independence. ★ This range of expressions has fascinated graphic designer Kit Hinrichs, who has amassed a collection of more than five thousand Stars and Stripes objects, from Civil War banners to Native American moccasins. ★ *100 American Flags* provides a glimpse of this spectacular collection and the stories behind each object.

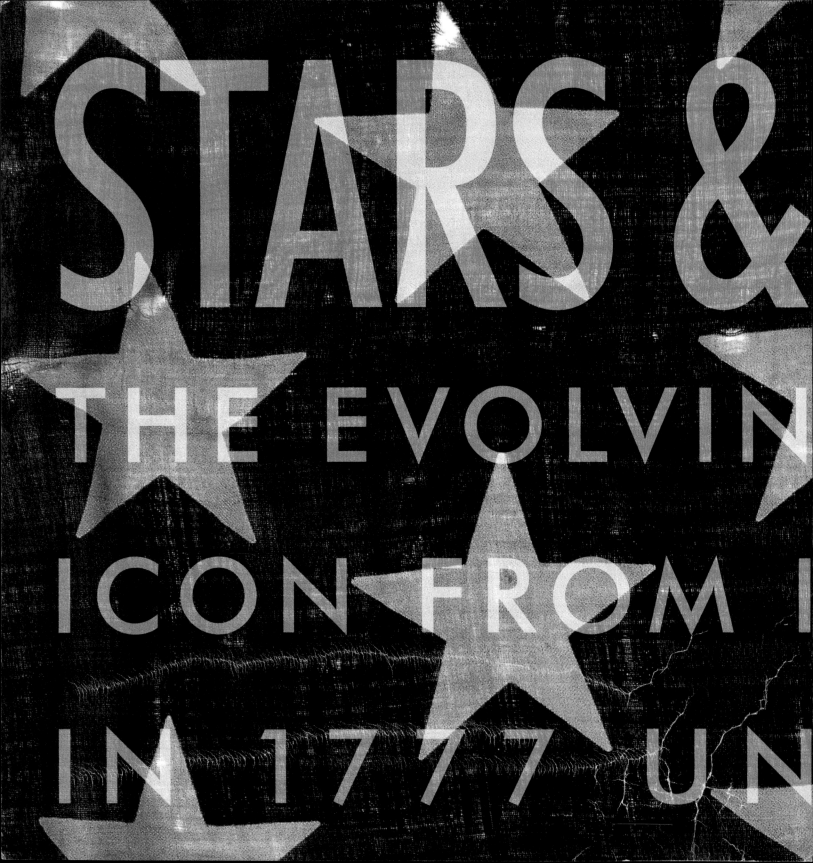

STARS &

THE EVOLVIN

ICON FROM

IN 1777 UN

Centennial Flag

In 1876, a flag
maker created this
flag to mark the one
hundredth anniversary
of the signing of
the Declaration of
Independence and
founding of the United
States. Although widely
known, the banner
is not considered an
official American flag
since it features eighty-
one stars instead of
thirty-eight, the number
of states in the Union
at the time.

Regimental Flag

Upon being disbanded,
the 71st New York
Volunteer Infantry
(also known as Sickles'
Brigade) created this
thirty-five-star flag
to commemorate the
major battles of the
Civil War in which the
regiment participated.

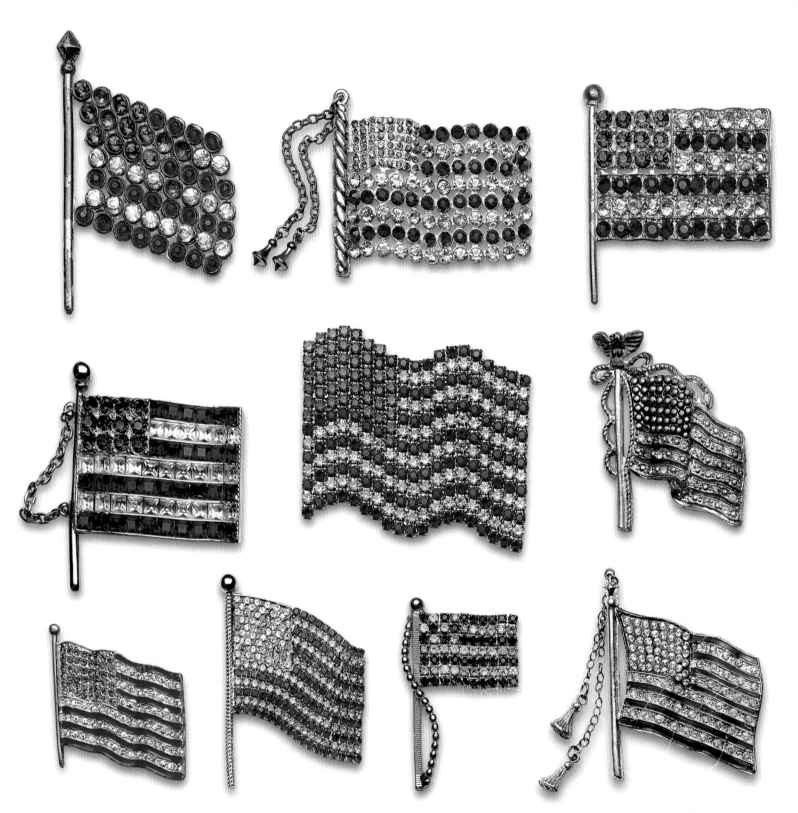

Assorted Patriotic Pins

Around 1891, two inventions—a machine that
could cut faceted glass and an automated metal
plating device—made the use of rhinestones
affordable for all types of costume jewelry.
The perfect accessory for patriotic occasions,
rhinestone flag pins of red, white, and blue
became the rage by the early twentieth century
and have remained popular ever since.

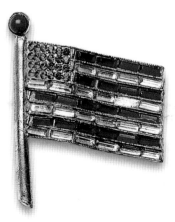

Crocheted Flag

During World War I
and II, even crochet
patterns printed in
women's magazines
featured the American
flag and wartime
slogans.

**Patriotic
Pillow Cover**

Crocheting was all the
rage in the early part of
the twentieth century,
reaching its peak around
the time of the First
World War. Patriotic
themes were particularly
popular then, since
more than four million
Americans—over
25 percent of the entire
U.S. male population
between the ages of
eighteen and thirty-
one—served in the
United States Army
during the Great War.

Stamp Cancellation Mark

The stamp cancellation mark used by the United States Postal Service in the late 1800s depicted a full waving flag. By the late 1920s, the postal service abbreviated the mark to just waving stripes, still used today.

Postage Flag

During World War II, an unknown artist assembled this flag from postage stamps and cancellation marks on envelopes. The stars in the canton bear the cancellation mark from the capital of each of the forty-eight states that were in the Union at the time.

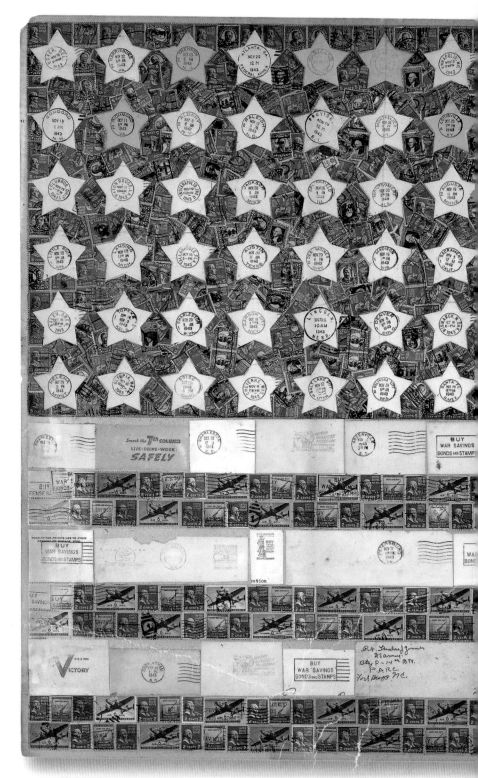

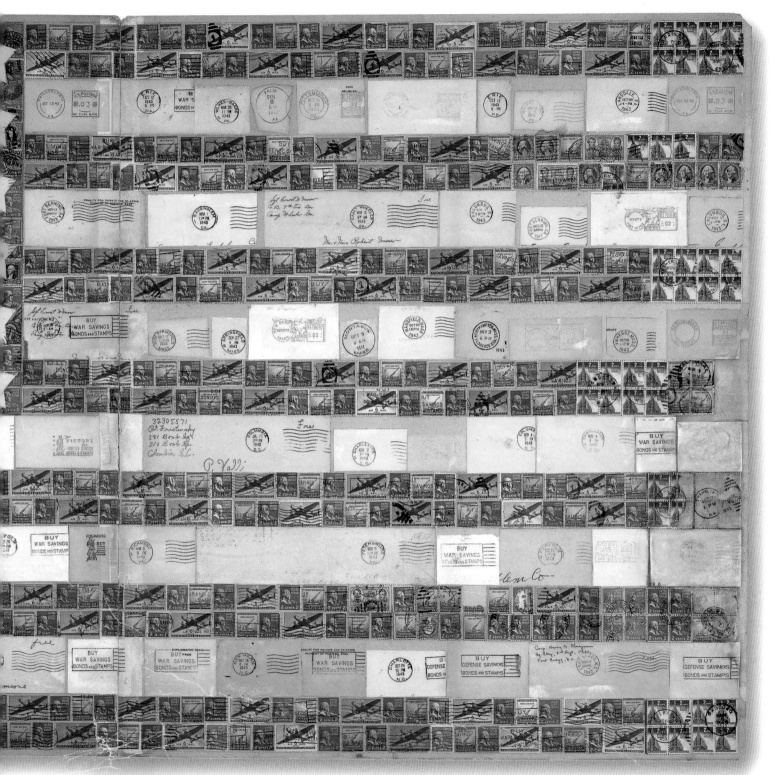

15

Flag Holder

Shaped much like the newel post of a staircase, this flag holder was used by stores in the late nineteenth century to display handheld flags for sale.

**Lady Liberty
Flag Holder**

The head of the Statue
of Liberty, presented
to the United States by
France in 1886, quickly
became a symbol
for American values
and an apt way for
shopkeepers to
display the flag.

The Non–Melting Pot Flag

For the bicentennial, Italian-born designer Massimo Vignelli, who lives in Manhattan, created this flag out of ethnic newspapers published in New York City. Vignelli portrays America not as a melting pot, but instead as a place that tolerates and supports the coexistence of different cultures and opinions.

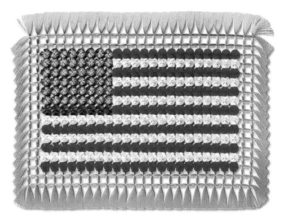

Tied-Silk Flag

In the 1930s, an unknown artist created a knotted-grid mat from gold silk thread, then tied and clipped red, white, and blue silk threads in a pattern that formed an image of the flag.

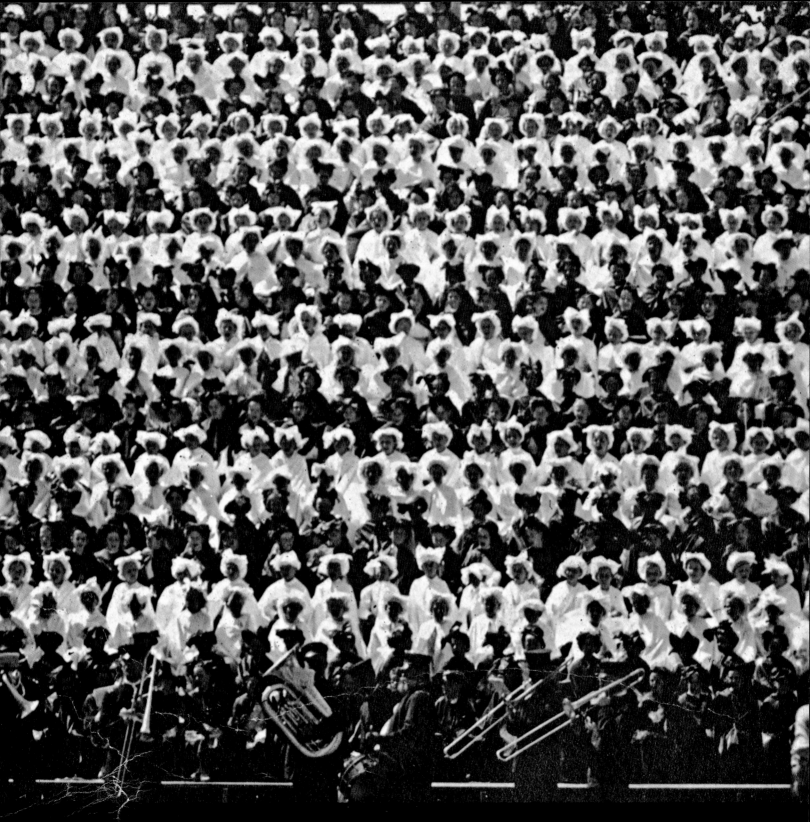

Grand Army of the Republic, celebrating the Union veterans of the Civil War, held in Salt Lake City, Utah, in August 1909. At the time, the G.A.R. had 220,600 members.

Fourth of July "Cap" Stick

Uncle Sam Party Hat

ICANNOTTELLALIE

Washington's Birthday Party Favor

Party Favor

Accordian Party Hat

Noisemaker

Clicker

22

Patriotic Party Paraphernalia

Noisemakers, party favors, and other objects with Stars and Stripes themes have been a part of every Fourth of July celebration since the country declared its independence from England in 1776.

Party Horn

Statue of Liberty Party Horn

Fourth of July Party Horn

Striped Party Horn

Parade Parasol

23

Scout Knife

The Stars and Stripes
figure prominently in
Boy Scout gear, along
with the teaching of
loyalty, patriotism, and
duty to country. Part
of Scout training is the
Pledge of Allegiance
and the proper
handling and respect
for the flag.

FLAG NO. 26

**Fund-Raising
Product**

Circa 1930, flag
manufacturers would
help Boy Scout troops
earn money to buy a
flag by providing them
with a free box of thirty
paper flag pins. The
scouts would in turn
sell the lapel pins for
ten cents a piece,
raising three dollars
per box—enough to
buy a 3- by 5-foot
cotton flag.

Needle Case

The top of this needle
kit is made with a petit
point stitch sewn onto
a felt back with a
beaded star.

Penny-Stitch Flag

About the time of
the Civil War, thrifty
homemakers began
using wool scrap
threads, sewn onto
a wool background,
to make decorative
coverings and wall
hangings. Pennies
were used as a circular
template, hence the
name *penny stitch*.

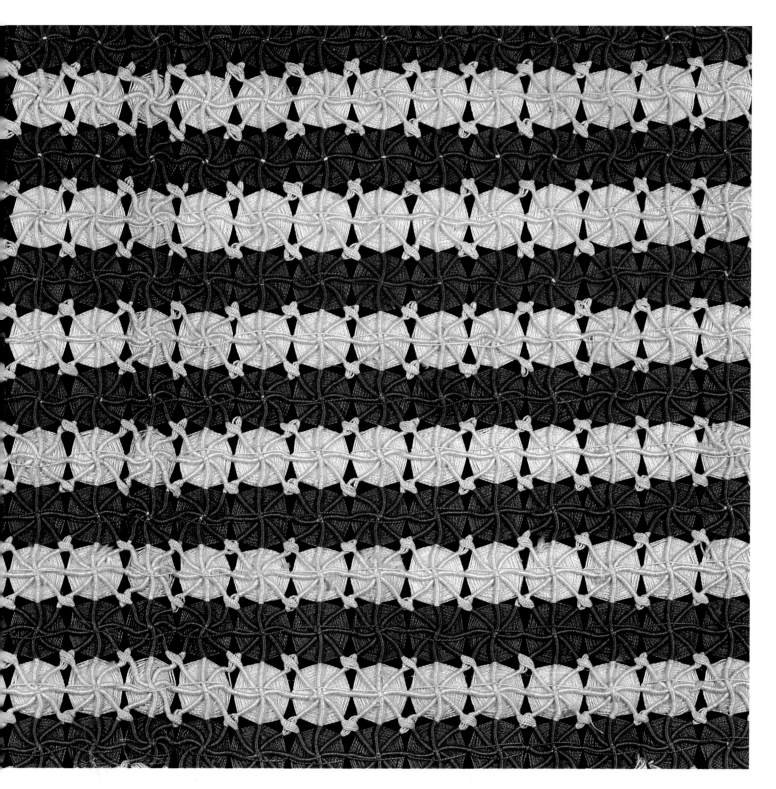

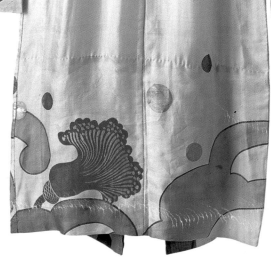

FLAG NO. 29

Friendship Kimono

This kimono, with flags
of both the United
States and Japan, was
probably created in
1912, the year that
Mayor Ozaki of Tokyo
presented President Taft
with three thousand
cherry blossom trees to
be planted along the
Potomac as a gesture
of friendship.

Patriotic Flag Dress

With four million Americans drafted into the Army during World War I, patriotic fervor ran high. A mother made this dress for her little girl to wear in a Fourth of July parade, circa 1917.

Cornhusk Bag

Designed for the tourist trade, this cornhusk bag was made by Pueblo Indians. Over the centuries, the Pueblos mastered the technique of wrapping the inner layer of cornhusks tightly around twine in a false embroidery technique. The husks would be dyed before being woven into bags, hats, and belts.

Navajo Chevrolet Flag Weaving

After the railroad reached Gallup, New Mexico, in 1882, Navajo weavers were encouraged to create rugs and patterns that appealed to non-Indian buyers. This rug once hung in a Chevrolet dealership in Gallup.

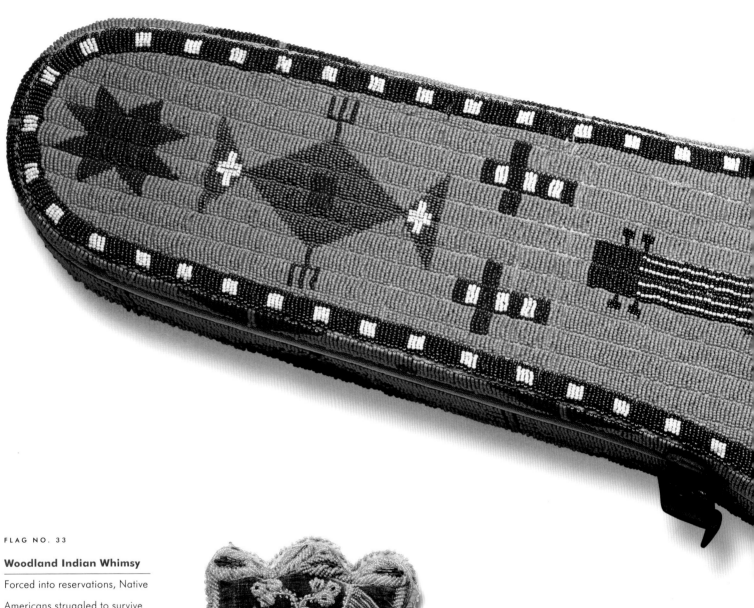

FLAG NO. 33

Woodland Indian Whimsy

Forced into reservations, Native Americans struggled to survive by creating craftwork for the non-Indian tourist trade. Around the early twentieth century, Woodland Indians made small beaded "whimsies" and sold them as souvenirs to tourists at Niagara Falls.

Beaded Flag Violin Case

This elaborately beaded violin case bears the initials R and B, which stand for the name of its owner, Rubin Bass. The symbolism and style of beading are representative of the work done by Brule Sioux in South Dakota. "Rubin Bass, Elk Falls, Feb. 11, 1891" is inscribed in deer hide on the back of the violin case.

Lakota
Gauntlet Gloves

Gauntlet gloves intended for commercial sales to non–Native Americans often featured realistic images rather than geometric designs. This pair of gloves was made by Lakota Indians during the reservation period that began in the late nineteenth century. The flag and domestic flower design was probably inspired by an image seen in a magazine.

Cheyenne Flag
Moccasins

Moccasins and other items such as armbands, breastplates, and pouches were often elaborately beaded by Cheyenne Indians. These moccasins feature lane or lazy stitch beadwork, a method by which eight or so beads are strung together then sewn tightly onto the animal hide surface.

Navajo Weaving

This Navajo flag weaving, representing a forty-nine-star grid, was created in 1959 to commemorate Alaska's entry into the Union. Forty-nine-star flags are relatively rare because of Hawaii's statehood the following year, raising the number of stars to fifty.

Second U.S. Calvary Guidon

Military units would fall into formation behind a guidon, or flag held aloft on a staff. This guidon was made for the Second U.S. Calvary, which fought in the Battle of Gettysburg in the Civil War as well as in Cuba during the Spanish-American War. Printed in 1890, this forty-two-star flag immediately became invalid due to the last-minute admission of Idaho as the forty-third state on July 3, 1890.

Tobacciana

Between 1890 and
1910, the American
Tobacco Trust waged
a major marketing
campaign to
monopolize all forms
of tobacco production.
The effort gave the
American Tobacco
Company control of
roughly 90 percent of
the tobacco production
in the United States
and Europe by 1903.
To woo smokers, the
company offered all
kinds of premiums,
including cigar "felts,"
cigarette cards, cigar
bands, and decorated
boxes. A favorite theme
was the Stars and
Stripes, which appealed
to the consumers'
sense of patriotism and
reminded them that
tobacco originated in
America, where the
best tobacco products
were still being
produced.

Presidential Cigar Bands

Thousands of cigar and cigarette brands existed in the early twentieth century. Tobacco companies vied for repeat customers by offering promotional items that they would want to collect, such as this series of presidential cigar bands.

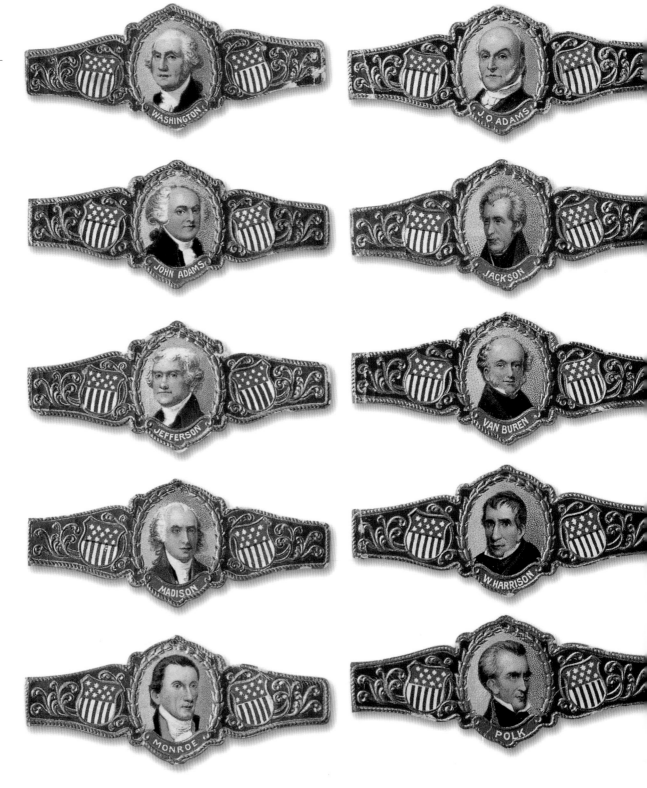

41

Victorian Trade Card

In the late nineteenth century, companies distributed decorative trade cards to promote their products. Sewing machine makers often issued cards featuring sweet little girls to imply that the machines made the task so easy that even a child could sew. Women and girls collected these cards to paste in their scrapbooks.

Fruit Can Label

Before Congress enacted an official code of flag etiquette in 1923, advertisers wrapped their brand image around the flag and all the patriotic values that the public connects to it.

Patriotic Airplane Livery

The Sopwith Camel—the plane flown by
Snoopy in the *Peanuts* comic strips—is
the best remembered military aircraft
of the First World War. Its agility in the
air accounted for destroying nearly
1,300 enemy aircraft. Produced in
Great Britain, the Sopwith Camel was
flown by two U.S. squadrons assigned
to the British forces, hence the Stars and
Stripes design of this model.

Flag Domino Tiles

The thirty-eight stars shown on the flag on the back side of these domino tiles offer a clue that the set was probably created sometime between 1877 and 1890, the year that five more states entered the Union.

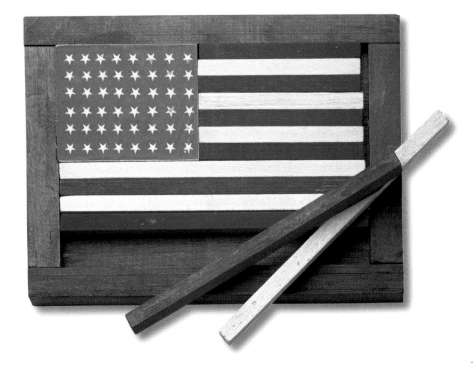

Stix Puzzle

Flag Stix puzzles helped young children increase their dexterity, identify familiar icons, and use logic to assemble the sticks to recreate the flag. Stix puzzles were available in the flags of many nations.

Flag Bearer Toy Soldiers

A flag bearer is an integral figure in every set of toy soldiers. Over the centuries, toy soldiers have been cast from metal, carved out of wood, and made from composition (sawdust and glue), and then hand-painted. Among collectors, the flag bearer is highly coveted for the symbolism of his role and the intricate workmanship required to reproduce the flag.

Mickey Mouse

The American flag and
Walt Disney's Mickey
Mouse are two of the
most recognizable
symbols of the United
States. The debut
of the first Mickey
Mouse film in 1928
made the animated
character an instant
star, with fans seeing
the best of America in
Mickey's optimism and
resourcefulness.

Bed Doll

Bed dolls were not
meant to be children's
playthings; rather,
they were used as
decorative accents.
As a result, they were
rather large and
delicate and were often
made of exceptionally
fine materials.

FLAG NO. 49

Uncle Sam Folding Fan

Over the years, flag fans have been made in a number of cylindrical forms, including the likeness of Uncle Sam. The body of this Uncle Sam is made of papier-mâché and the head is of clay.

52

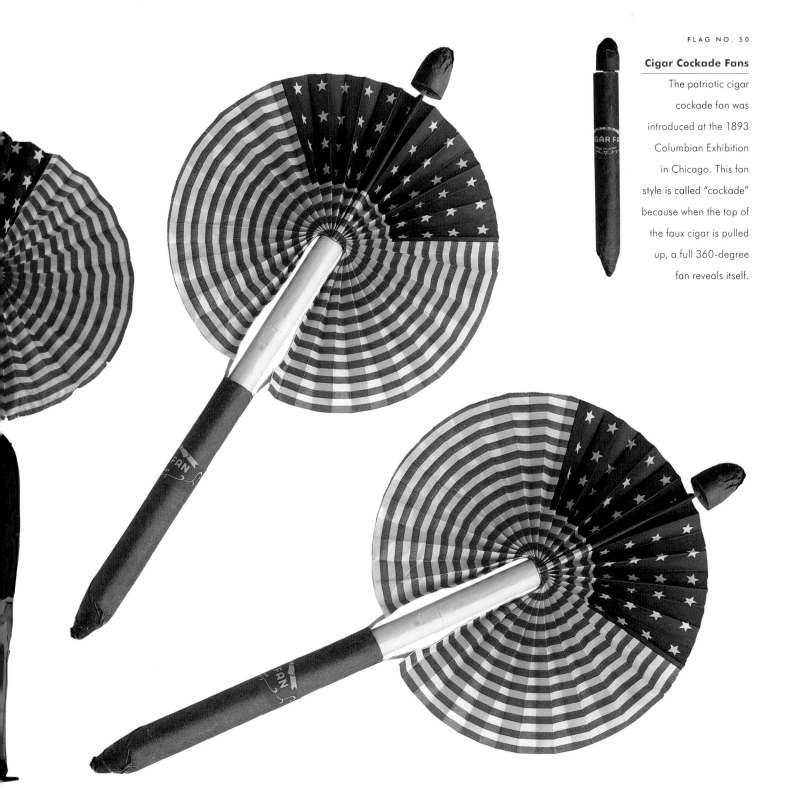

Cigar Cockade Fans

The patriotic cigar cockade fan was introduced at the 1893 Columbian Exhibition in Chicago. This fan style is called "cockade" because when the top of the faux cigar is pulled up, a full 360-degree fan reveals itself.

Uncle Sam Bank

David and Susan Kirk
created this mechanical
Uncle Sam bank in
the late 1970s. Uncle
Sam's eyes recede and
his tongue extends to
receive the coins. David
Kirk is the creator of the
much-loved Miss Spider
children's book series.

Homemade Puzzle

Crafted from scrap
materials, this
homemade puzzle is
designed to teach a
young child how to
match sizes, shapes,
and colors.

Pencil Assemblage

For an American
Institute of Graphic Arts
exhibition and auction,
Texas-based graphic
designer Chris Hill
created this original
piece out of twenty-four
hundred red, white, and
blue pencils.

Pencil Box

Uncle Sam and the
Stars and Stripes
decorate this pencil
container designed for
schoolchildren.

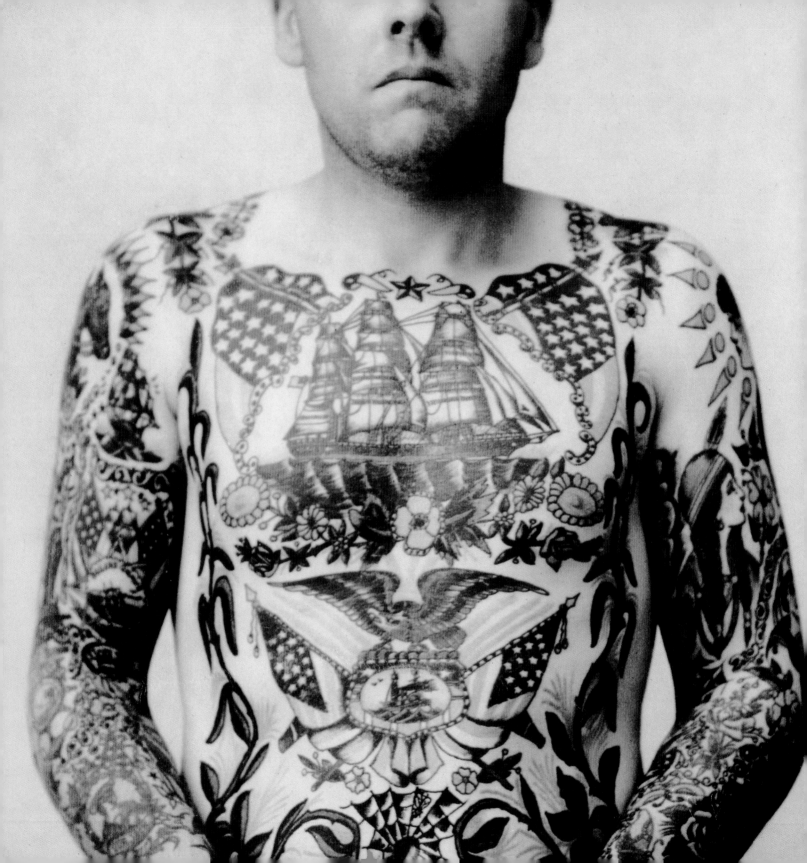

Tattooed Sailor

Sailor William Ray, who served in the United
States Navy circa September 1917, according to
the date tattooed on his back, embellished his
torso and arms with patriotic images and nautical
themes. His tattoo art was photographed and
printed as postcards.

Junior Mechanics Flag

The Junior Order of United American Mechanics, an anti-immigrant fraternal organization formed in Germantown, Pennsylvania, in 1853, centered its symbol—a compass and mason's square framing labor's arm and hammer—amid the flag's canton of stars.

**Twenty-Nine-
Star Flag**

This twenty-nine-star
parade flag from
1847 presents the
stars in a medallion
configuration with the
center star larger than
the others. Printed on
buckram, the flag was
probably produced
for use in James K.
Polk's campaign for
president.

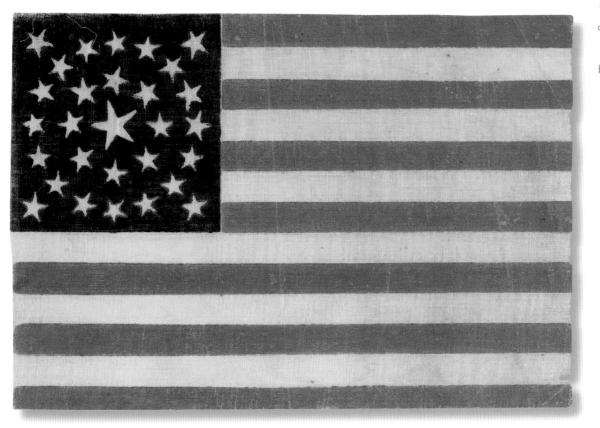

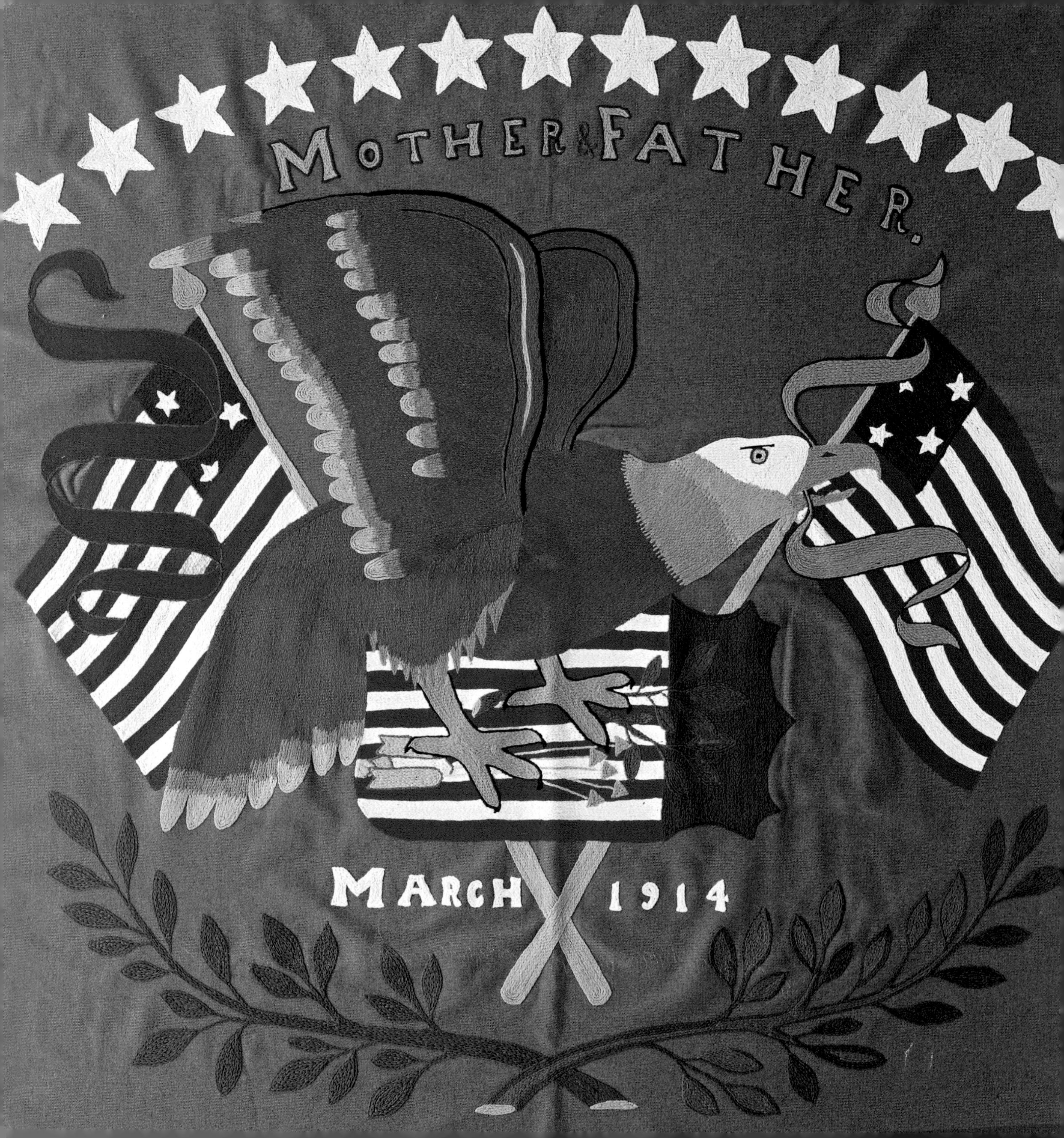
MOTHER & FATHER.
MARCH 1914

Army Blanket

On the eve of the
United States's entry
into the First World
War, a soldier whose
initials were E. H.
embroidered patriotic
images on an army
blanket for his parents.

**Pearl Harbor
Blanket**

A mother's grief
for a son killed on
the USS *Arizona* in
1941 is expressed
on this crocheted
blanket, which shows
battleships, warplanes,
machine guns, and
pistols, along with
the exact time of
the attack on
Pearl Harbor.

FLAG NO. 61

Hickam Field Flag

This flag flew over
Hickam Field, adjacent
to the Pearl Harbor
U.S. naval base in
Hawaii. The slogan
on the flag was the
rallying cry in the war
against Japan and
also was used to
encourage citizens to
buy war bonds.

Admiral Dewey Pin

This pin and silk flag
featuring a brass bust
of Admiral George
Dewey commemorated
the Navy's Great White
Fleet. As president of
the General Board
of the Navy, Dewey
was instrumental in
developing a greater
naval presence for the
United States, including
a global voyage of the
Great White Fleet in
1907 to demonstrate
America's sea power.

**Eagle, Flag,
and Shield Label**

After defeating the
Spanish fleet in the
Battle of Manila during
the Spanish-American
War of 1898, Admiral
George Dewey was
viewed as a national
hero, with his picture
even appearing on
a whiskey flask. His
popularity prompted
him to run for president
in 1900, but he quickly
withdrew his candidacy.

Woven Ribbons

Starting in 1862, political
ribbons began featuring
finely detailed words and
images thanks to a silk-
weaving technique called
Stevengraph, invented
by the English ribbon
maker Thomas Stevens
using a Jacquard loom.
The first Stevengraphs
appeared as bookmarks,
and were later followed
by other formats such as
postcards. This selection
includes Stevengraphs
as well as traditional
printed, stamped, and
embroidered ribbons.

ADELPHIA

NATIONAL

IBITION

AND FRANCE

FOR EVER

NNIAL 1876

ENIR

VENIR.
of
RSON, N.J.

MALICE TOWA
HARITY FOR
SS IN THE RIGH
US TO SEE THE
FINISH THE WORK WE
D UP THE NATION'S
CARE FOR HIM WHO
NE THE BATTLE, AN
OW AND HIS ORPHA
L WHICH MAY ACH
HERISH A JUST AND
EACE AMONG OU
AND WITH
NATIONS.

THE FATHER
OF HIS
Country
E PLURIBUS UNUM

TWENTIE
NATIONA
ENCAMPM

SAN FRANCISCO
1886

AMERICAN
BOWLING
CONGRESS
27th
INTERNATIONAL
TOURNAMENT
PEORIA, ILL.
Mar. 5 to Apr. 10
1927

Handlebar Ornament

Airplanes were recent inventions when this pre–World War I bicycle ornament was created. It was designed to fly merrily from its mount on the handlebar, while the propeller spun.

Soldiers' Portraits

Soldiers shipping off for the First World War would sit for portraits that were printed with a decorative frame as a single celluloid unit. The unbreakable frames made it easy to send the portraits back to families at home.

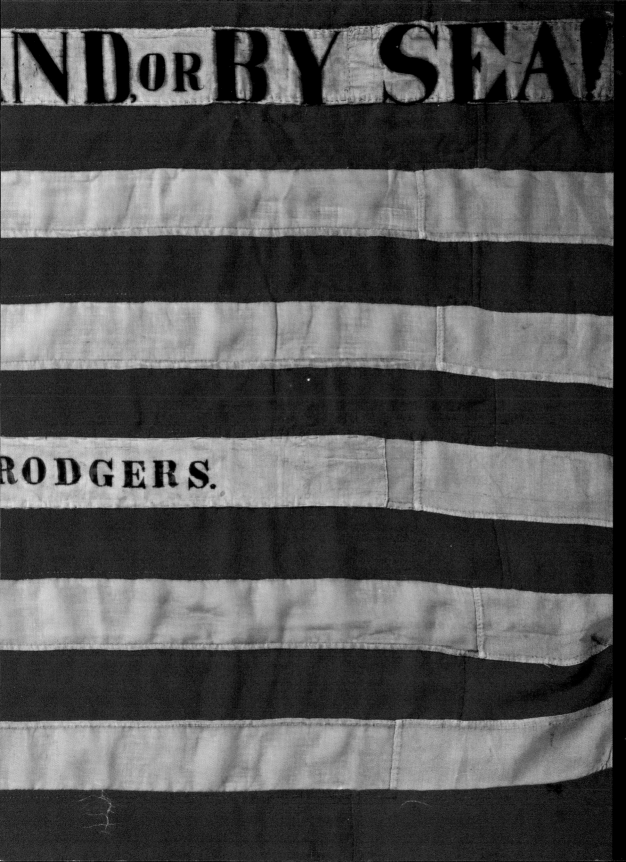

ND, OR BY SEA!

RODGERS.

Rodgers's
Battle Flag

This flag flew on ships
commanded by Admiral
John Rodgers during
the Civil War and the
Korean Conflict of
1871. The banner first
saw action in 1861
when then-Captain
Rodgers's ship came
under cannon fire
from Confederate
troops. For his bravery,
Rodgers was promoted
to rear admiral and
presented with the
flag. In 1871, he was
put in charge of the
Asiatic Fleet, which
fought several battles in
Korea. After the signing
of the Korean treaty,
Rodgers presented the
flag to a lieutenant
who had risked his life
rescuing it during the
storming of a fort on
the Seoul River.

Poker Chips

National pride ran
high during America's
centennial celebrations
in 1876. Manufacturers
embellished all manner
of products with
the American flag,
including these clay
poker chips.

**Victory
Playing Cards**

Although playing cards
was a diversion from
the war, the cause
was never far from
anyone's mind. During
World War II, card
decks usually pictured
patriotic themes. Here,
Hitler and Mussolini
are the Jokers.

Commemorative Spoons

Sold at world's fairs, in tourist gift shops, and at special events, commemorative spoons have been popular collectibles for more than a century. Patriotic motifs have been perennial best-sellers.

Eagle and Shield, Cloisonné

Crossed Flags, Silver and Enamel

Sesquicentennial, Sterling Silver and Enamel

Battleship Maine, Silver and Enamel

Oklahoma, Silver and Enamel

Battleship Maine, Silver and Enamel

Eagle and Shield, Etched Silver and Cloisonné

Army and Navy, Gold Plate and Enamel

Panama Canal, Silver and Cloisonné

Forty-Eight-Star Flag, Sterling Silver and Enamel

Uncle Sam, Silver and Cloisonné

Chicago, Silver and Enamel

Ladies' Compacts

The designs for ladies'
compacts ranged from
austere brass and wood
from World War I
and World War II to
glamorous rhinestone
and elegant enamel,
put out for the nation's
bicentennial.

FLAG NO. 72

Shotgun Shell Case

A one-of-a-kind
piece, this shotgun
shell case was
lovingly inlaid with
hunting dogs and
a forty-eight-star
flag by an amateur
woodworker in
the 1940s.

Weather Vanes

Weather vanes were
once a common sight
on barns across rural
America. The nation's
flag was a popular
icon because its broad,
flat surface easily
caught the wind. These
printed-tin vanes date
from World War I and
World War II. The holes
in some of the stars
were made by farm
boys using the fixtures
for target practice.

"Solid as the Oak" Pillow Cover

This embroidered pillow case from around 1910 was probably made from a pattern that appeared in a women's magazine or was printed on cloth to be individually stitched at home.

SOLID
as the
OAK

is
our own

U·S·A·

Outsider Art Flag

This primitive drawing on tin is one of many pieces made by R. A. Miller, a Georgia farmer and cotton mill worker. Although stricken by glaucoma, he continues as one of the better known outsider artists, painting tin cutouts and whirligigs often with patriotic themes.

Crazy Quilt

Crazy quilts became the rage after the Philadelphia Centennial Exposition of 1876. A way for women to show off their stitching skills, these quilts were typically assembled from silk, velvet, and broad fabrics cut in random shapes. Their design often incorporated bits of cultural lore, patriotic symbols, and family history.

McKinley Quilt

This quilt, constructed of uncut flags and flag bunting, was made in memory of William McKinley, who became president of the United States in 1897 and was assassinated by an anarchist named Leon Czolgosz in 1901. The initials W. R. H. are those of the quilt maker.

Centennial Quilt

Created to mark the nation's centennial, this quilt features thirty-six-star flags, even though thirty-eight states were officially part of the Union at the time.

Toy Biplane

This tin toy biplane was made in Japan prior to World War II for sale in the U.S. market.

FLAG NO. 80

Lucky Lindy Folk Art Flag

This one-of-a-kind chenille piece by José Santos of New Rochelle, New York, commemorates the first nonstop east and west crossing of the Atlantic by American and French flyers. Rife with information, the wall hanging incorporates photographs of Charles Lindbergh and the two French pilots and their national flags, with names and flight records embroidered along the border.

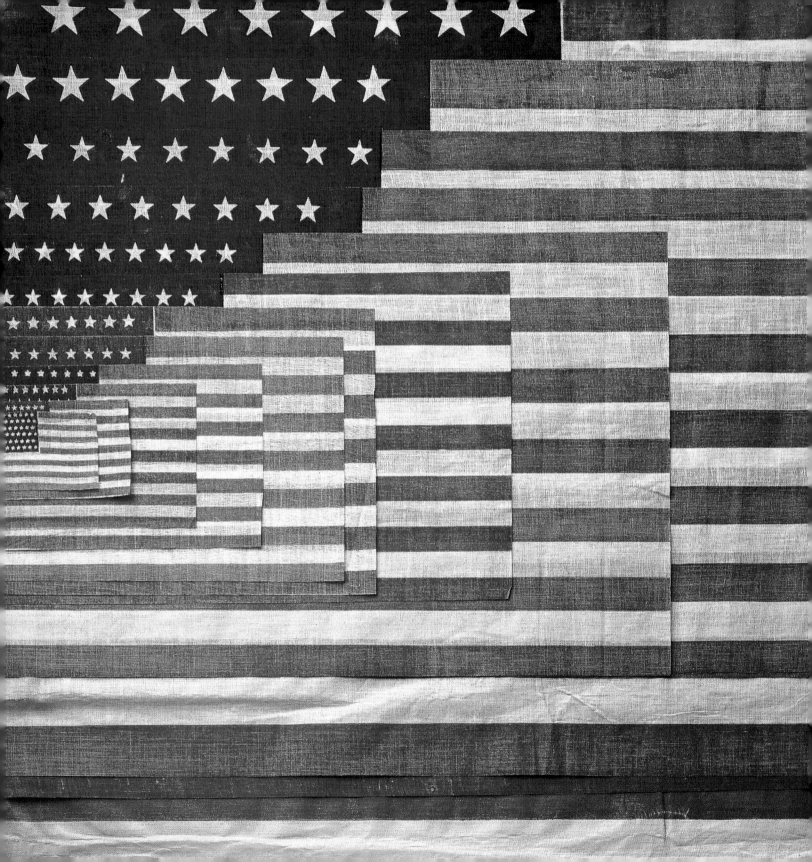

FLAG NO. 81

Salesman's Sampler

Produced in 1912 to
introduce the new
forty-eight-star flag,
this sampler was used
by flag salesmen to
show customers the
thirteen different sizes
of flags the company
had available.

**Red Star Line
Folding Fan**

This is a promotional fan from the Red Star Line shipping company, which between 1873 and 1935 transported almost three million passengers from Antwerp, Belgium, to North America. Many immigrants who passed through New York's Ellis Island came here on a Red Star vessel.

Lands' End Quilt

Commissioned by
Lands' End to create
a flag quilt design for
the cover of its catalog,
graphic designer
and flag collector
Kit Hinrichs made an
assemblage from his
favorite nineteenth
century flag designs.
Quilting artist Sonya
Lee Barrington then
hand-dyed the fabric,
assembled the pieces,
and quilted Hinrichs's
design into a wall
hanging.

**Nevada
Statehood Quilt**

A ten-woman quilting
circle commemorated
Nevada's entry as the
thirty-sixth state in the
Union by sewing this
satin thirty-six-star flag
quilt in a log cabin
pattern. The quilt later
hung in the offices of
the chief of police in
San Francisco.

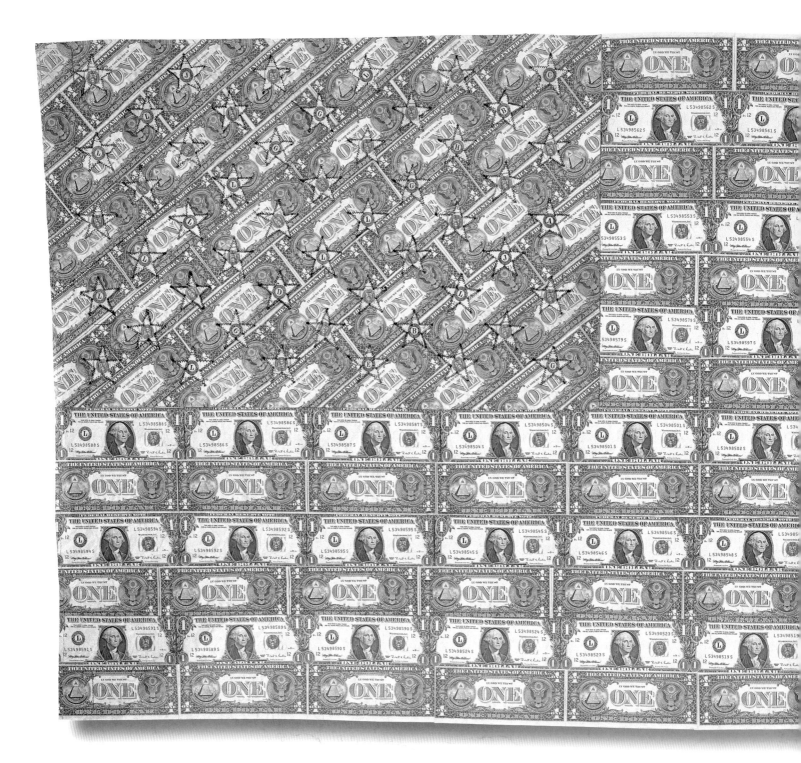

94

Flag Money Clip

Although official flag
etiquette bans the
use of the American
flag for advertising
purposes, it does not
forbid displaying it on
all kinds of products,
including money clips.

FLAG NO. 85

Dollar Flag

Artist Ray Beldner
is known for turning
money into art, in
this case sewing
157 one-dollar bills
together, alternating
front and back sides,
to create this American
flag. His series titled
"Counterfeit" remakes
masterpieces by
Duchamp, Warhol,
and others from U.S.
currency.

**Greek and
American Flags**

A Greek immigrant
made this folksy art
piece from beads wired
to a painted vegetable
crate to celebrate the
friendship between
Greece and the United
States. The plaque
bears the Greek
inscription "liberty."

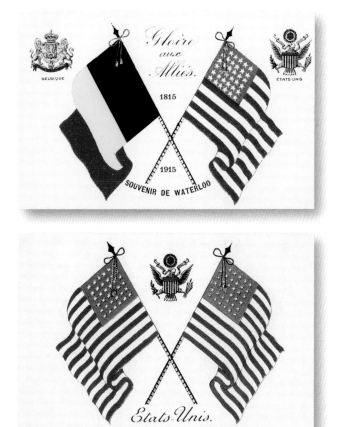

**World War I
Postcards**

These postcards were
produced in Belgium
during the First World
War. They feature the
flags of Allied nations
and the U.S. flag.

FLAG NO. 90

Peace Flag

Over the years,
different groups have
substituted the Stars
and Stripes on the flag
with other symbols,
including the peace
sign, to support
their causes.

FLAG NO. 91

Anti-War Placard

During the Vietnam
War, this placard,
featuring silhouettes of
rifles and warplanes,
was produced on
the campus of the
University of California
at Berkeley.

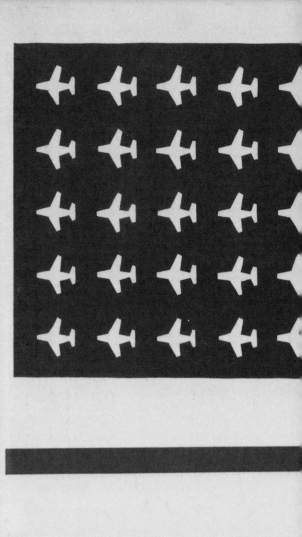

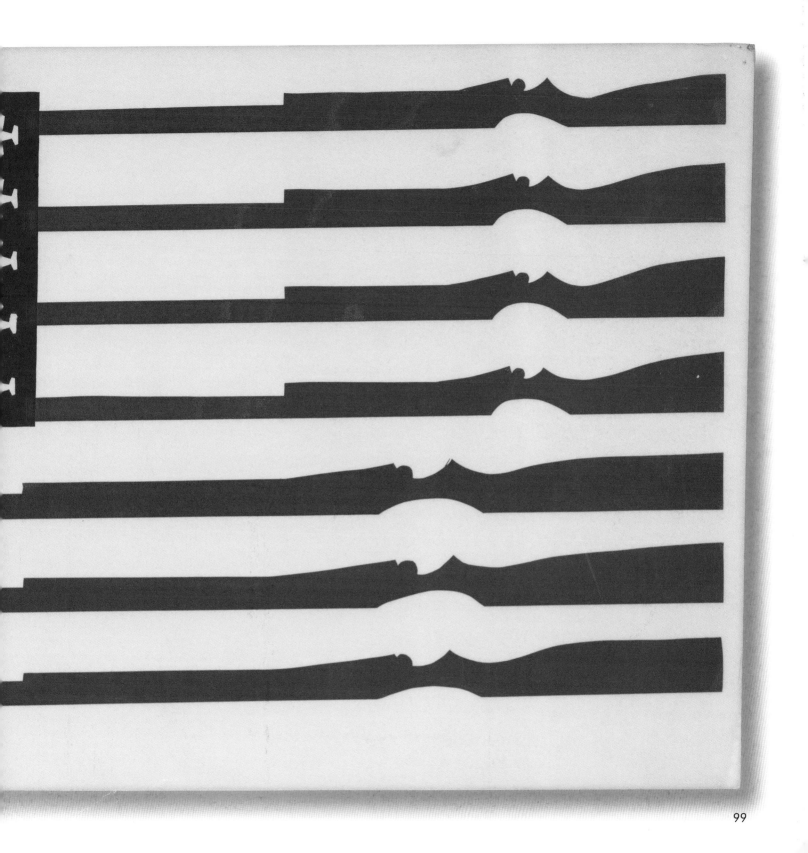

Union Shield

This wooden emblem
is believed to be the
shield for a presidential
campaign train at
the beginning of the
twentieth century.

**Iroquois
Plateau Pouch**

During the early
reservation period
between 1880 and
1920, beadwork arts
flourished among
Plateau people and
were bought by
tourists, collectors,
and museums.

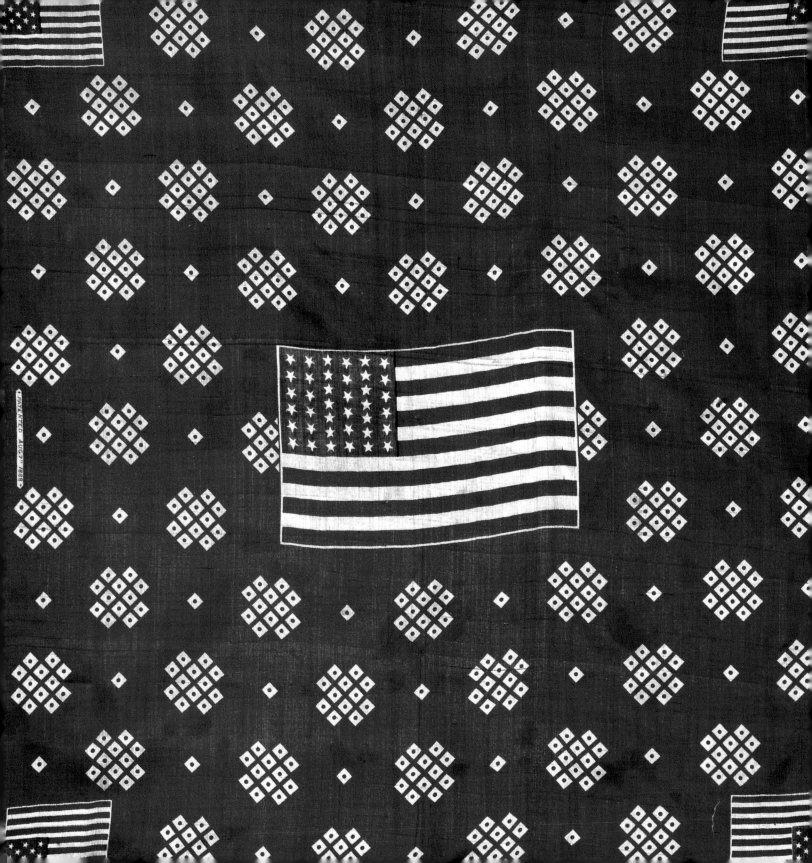

**Red Flag
Handkerchief**

Although this flag
handkerchief has
thirty-six stars,
corresponding to 1865,
it was actually created
in 1888 and may
have coincided with
Benjamin Harrison's
run for the presidency.

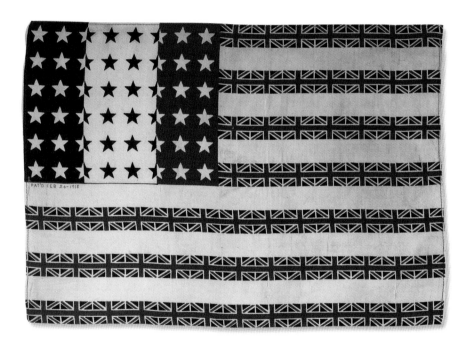

**Franco-Anglo-
American Alliance
"Humanity Flag"**

To represent the
Allied powers—Great
Britain, France, and
the United States—of
the First World War,
Albert Hewitt of Mount
Vernon, New York,
designed and patented
a variation of the
Stars and Stripes,
turning the usual blue
canton into the French
Tricolor and substituting
rows of the British
Union Jack for the red
stripes. He named his
amalgamation the
"humanity flag."

Patriotic Buttons

The late 1890s saw the introduction of inexpensive patriotic buttons made by placing a thin piece of celluloid protective covering over printed paper and then wrapping it around a metal disk.

Benjamin Harrison Handkerchief

With thirty-eight states in the Union when Benjamin Harrison ran for president in 1888, campaigning had become a cross-continental effort. This made political giveaways such as this printed handkerchief an essential for promoting the party platform.

Political Handkerchiefs

Engraved copper cylinders enabled whole lengths of bleached cotton cloth and silk to be printed quickly and inexpensively. Campaign handkerchiefs were then mass produced and blanketed late nineteenth century America.

Uncle Sam Postcard

Popular during the
early twentieth century,
a uniquely Chinese
art form of watercolor
and collage was used
to create this image
of Uncle Sam. Uncle
Sam's attire is made
entirely out of canceled
U.S. stamps.

FLAG NO. 100

Living Flag

During and shortly after
the First World War,
a young photographer
named Arthur S. Mole
and his partner,
John D. Thomas, visited
military camps around
the country and created
dozens of "living
photographs." In 1917,
ten thousand cadets
(all saluting) at the
United States Naval
Training Station in
Great Lakes, Illinois,
were assembled on
the parade ground for
this photograph. Mole
stood on an eighty-foot
tower that his assistants
constructed to gain the
proper perspective for
his picture.

A Chronological History

The American flag has changed frequently and dramatically since the Continental Congress resolved on June 14, 1777 "that the flag of the United States be thirteen stripes, alternate red and white; that the Union be thirteen stars, white in a blue field representing a new constellation." The vague wording left much room for graphic interpretation, encouraged further by two Congressional acts. In 1795, Congress decreed that a single star and single stripe be added whenever a new state joined the Union. In 1818, Congress changed its mind, reverting back to thirteen horizontal stripes, alternating red and white, to symbolize the original colonies, with each state represented by a single star. The new star would be added on the Fourth of July following a state's admission to the Union. In 1912, Congress finally legislated official graphic standards for how the flag must appear. Presented here is a chronology of state admissions and one example of how the flag was graphically interpreted at that time.

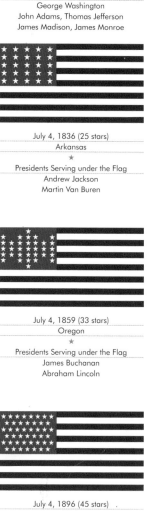

June 14, 1777 (13 stars)
Delaware
Pennsylvania
New Jersey
Georgia
Connecticut
Massachusetts
Maryland
South Carolina
New Hampshire
Virginia
New York
North Carolina
Rhode Island
★
President Serving under the Flag
George Washington

May 1, 1795 (15 stars)
Vermont
Kentucky
★
Presidents Serving under the Flag
George Washington
John Adams, Thomas Jefferson
James Madison, James Monroe

July 4, 1836 (25 stars)
Arkansas
★
Presidents Serving under the Flag
Andrew Jackson
Martin Van Buren

July 4, 1848 (30 stars)
Wisconsin
★
Presidents Serving under the Flag
James K. Polk
Zachary Taylor
Millard Fillmore

July 4, 1851 (31 stars)
California
★
Presidents Serving under the Flag
Millard Fillmore
Franklin Pierce
James Buchanan

July 4, 1858 (32 stars)
Minnesota
★
President Serving under the Flag
James Buchanan

July 4, 1859 (33 stars)
Oregon
★
Presidents Serving under the Flag
James Buchanan
Abraham Lincoln

July 4, 1877 (38 stars)
Colorado
★
Presidents Serving under the Flag
Rutherford B. Hayes, James Garfield
Chester Alan Arthur, Grover Cleveland
Benjamin Harrison

July 4, 1890 (43 stars)
North Dakota
South Dakota
Montana
Washington
Idaho
★
President Serving under the Flag
Benjamin Harrison

July 4, 1891 (44 stars)
Wyoming
★
Presidents Serving under the Flag
Benjamin Harrison
Grover Cleveland

July 4, 1896 (45 stars)
Utah
★
Presidents Serving under the Flag
Grover Cleveland
William McKinley
Theodore Roosevelt

April 13, 1818 (20 stars)
Tennessee, Ohio
Louisiana, Indiana
Mississippi
★
President Serving under the Flag
James Monroe

July 4, 1819 (21 stars)
Illinois
★
President Serving under the Flag
James Monroe

July 4, 1820 (23 stars)
Alabama
Maine
★
President Serving under the Flag
James Monroe

July 4, 1822 (24 stars)
Missouri
★
Presidents Serving under the Flag
James Monroe
John Quincy Adams
Andrew Jackson

July 4, 1837 (26 stars)
Michigan
★
Presidents Serving under the Flag
Martin Van Buren
William Henry Harrison
John Tyler
James K. Polk

July 4, 1845 (27 stars)
Florida
★
President Serving under the Flag
James K. Polk

July 4, 1846 (28 stars)
Texas
★
President Serving under the Flag
James K. Polk

July 4, 1847 (29 stars)
Iowa
★
President Serving under the Flag
James K. Polk

July 4, 1861 (34 stars)
Kansas
★
President Serving under the Flag
Abraham Lincoln

July 4, 1863 (35 stars)
West Virginia
★
Presidents Serving under the Flag
Abraham Lincoln
Andrew Johnson

July 4, 1865 (36 stars)
Nevada
★
President Serving under the Flag
Andrew Johnson

July 4, 1867 (37 stars)
Nebraska
★
Presidents Serving under the Flag
Andrew Johnson
Ulysses S. Grant
Rutherford B. Hayes

July 4, 1908 (46 stars)
Oklahoma
★
Presidents Serving under the Flag
Theodore Roosevelt
William Howard Taft

July 4, 1912 (48 stars)
New Mexico
Arizona
★
Presidents Serving under the Flag
William Howard Taft, Woodrow Wilson
Warren G. Harding, Calvin Coolidge
Herbert Hoover, Franklin D. Roosevelt
Harry S. Truman, Dwight D. Eisenhower

July 4, 1959 (49 stars)
Alaska
★
President Serving under the Flag
Dwight D. Eisenhower

July 4, 1960 (50 stars)
Hawaii
★
Presidents Serving under the Flag
Dwight D. Eisenhower, John F. Kennedy
Lyndon Johnson, Richard Nixon
Gerald Ford, Jimmy Carter
Ronald Reagan, George H. W. Bush
William Clinton, George W. Bush

SPECIAL THANKS

Thanks to Aaron Wehner and Brie Mazurek at Ten Speed Press, and to Gloria Hiek
for her dedication to designing and producing this book.

CREDITS

Ten Speed Press
PO Box 7123
Berkeley, California 94707
www.tenspeed.com

Distributed in Australia by Simon and Schuster Australia, in Canada
by Ten Speed Press Canada, in New Zealand by Southern Publishers Group,
in South Africa by Real Books, and in the United Kingdom and
Europe by Publishers Group UK.

Cover and text design by Kit Hinrichs/Pentagram
Much of the material in this book has been previously published in *Long May She Wave*
(Ten Speed Press, 2001; 978-1-58008-240-2).

Library of Congress Cataloging-in-Publication Data
Hinrichs, Kit. 100 American flags : a unique collection of Old Glory memorabilia / collection &
design by Kit Hinrichs ; text by Delphine Hirasuna ; photography by Terry Heffernan.
"Much of the material in this book has been previously published in *Long May She Wave*."
Summary: "A full-color photographic book presenting 100 American flag artifacts, artworks, and
memorabilia from one of the world's most eminent collections"—Provided by publisher.
p. cm.
ISBN-13: 978-1-58008-920-3
ISBN-10: 1-58008-920-8   7540
1. Flags in art. 2. Art, American—Pictorial works. 3. Flags—United States—Pictorial works.
4. Hinrichs, Kit—Art collections—Pictorial works. 5. Art—Private collections—United States—Pictorial works.
I. Hirasuna, Delphine, 1946– II. Heffernan, Terry. III. Title. IV. Title: One hundred American flags.
N8217.F55H5595 2008 929.9'20973—dc22 2007049871

Printed in Singapore
First printing, 2008
1 2 3 4 5 6 7 8 9 10 — 12 11 10 09 08